Wild Ducks and Geese of North America

By Sandra Romashko

Illustrated by Russ Smiley

Windward Publishing, Inc.

105 NE 25th St.   P.O. Box 371005   Miami, Fl. 33137

Other books by the author:
The Shell Book
Shark: Lord of the Sea
Living Coral
The Sportfisherman's Handbook
The Coral Book
Savory Shellfish of North America
Birds of the Water, Sea and Shore

ISBN 0-89317-018-6
Library of Congress No. 77-81167
1 3 5 7 9 10 8 6 4 2
Printed in the United States of America

Contents

Introduction

Ducks, geese and swans make up the informal grouping of birds we commonly refer to as "waterfowl". The two North American species of swans, the trumpeter swan, *Olor buccinator,* and the whistling swan, *Olor columbianus,* are not included here since they are strictly protected by law and thus are not legally gamebirds.

The forty-five species of ducks and geese included in this text are, along with the swans, all of the living species of waterfowl found in North America. World-wide, there are 8660 living species of birds identified and an estimated 100 species unidentified. Of this number, 147 species are members of the duck family, family *Anatidae,* which are the ducks, geese and swans.

Waterfowl have several general characteristics in common.

1. They have a flattened bill with both upper and lower mandibles edged with small tooth-like serrations called *lamellae.*
2. Each foot has four toes, the first three of which are webbed and the fourth is a small unwebbed toe.
3. They have short, wide-set, and powerful legs.
4. Their body is covered with a heavy coat of down which is covered by thick feathers.
5. All species are unable to fly for some period of time each year when they molt, since all of the flight feathers are molted at once.
6. They have well insulated, bouyant bodies.
7. Their young are covered with down and can swim shortly after hatching.

Their nests are usually on the ground, but some are built in holes or trees. Down from the female's breast usually lines the nest which normally contains from 2 to 16 eggs. Eggs can be white, buff, or greenish and can be incubated by either parent. The chicks are covered with down at birth.

All members of this family are excellent flyers and in this respect are superior to other families of birds. Some ducks have had their speeds recorded at over 70 mph, but the usual flying speed is between 20-40 mph, and under certain conditions, 40-60 mph. Certain species can fly more than 100 miles a day and can fly as far as 4000 miles during migration. Waterfowl normally fly at low altitudes, but some geese fly at levels of 10,000 feet during migration, and the snow goose flies at over 25,000 feet.

All waterfowl are flightless for some period of time during the breeding season (spring-summer). Corresponding to the time the eggs are being incubated, both sexes molt—including all wing feathers. During this molt, the male duck sheds his bright colorful plumage, which is replaced by the drab "female-type" colored feathers. This coloration, when the drake resembles the female duck, is known as the eclipse plumage and presumably helps camouflage him during this flightless period. After this molt is complete a second molt begins and gradually over a period of several months, the colorful "breeding plumage" of the male duck is restored. This plumage is the one usually appearing in paintings of ducks.

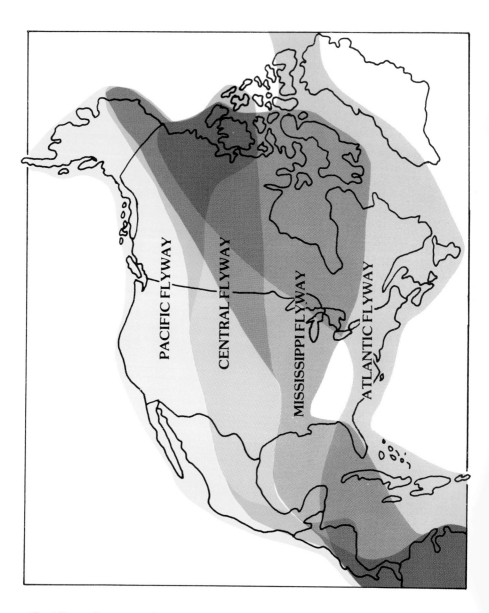

To aid law enforcement, flyway boundaries have been adjusted to state lines in the United States. The Pacific Flyway extends from the Pacific coast to the eastern borders of Idaho, Utah, and Arizona. The Central Flyway extends from Pacific Flyway to the eastern borders of North Dakota, South Dakota, Nebraska, Kansas, Oklahoma, and Texas. The Mississippi Flyway extends to the eastern borders of Ohio, Kentucky, Tennessee, and Alabama; the Atlantic Flyway extends to the Atlantic coast.

BODY STRUCTURE (GOOSE)

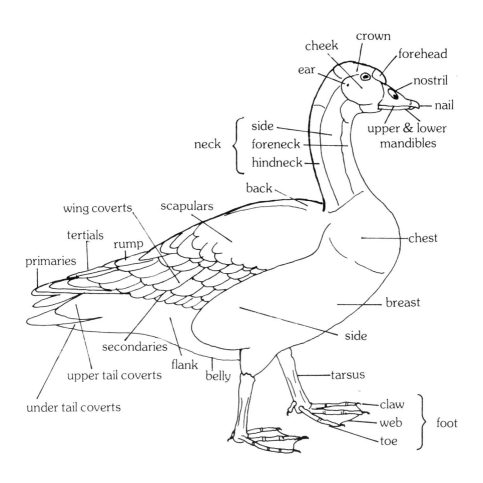

Classification of Waterfowl

Kingdom: *Animal*
Phylum: *Chordata*
Class: *Aves*
Order: *Anseriformes*
Family: *Anatidae*
(sub-family or tribe)
Genus:
Species: } 147 species world-wide
(sub-species or race)

WING STRUCTURE (DUCK)

Wing From Above

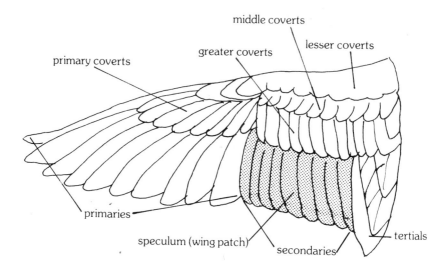

middle coverts

greater coverts

lesser coverts

primary coverts

primaries

speculum (wing patch)

secondaries

tertials

Wing From Below

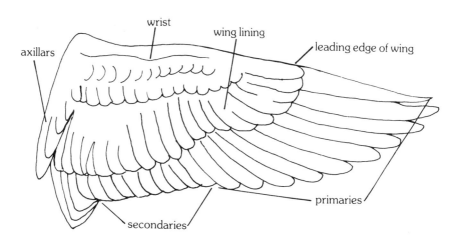

wrist

wing lining

leading edge of wing

axillars

primaries

secondaries

Waterfowl migrate along four major paths or flyways in North America. These flyways are not rigid, overlapping at the north and south extremes. They are best defined in the United States. Certain populations of birds migrate together along the same flyway year after year. This habit makes these birds more vulnerable to overshooting since their location can be predicted by hunters. Concentrations of waterfowl in the flyways may vary among the four flyways and from year to year depending on the availability of food, the weather, the number of young produced, and the amount of hunting. Hunting regulations on migrating game-birds are described for each of the flyways; thus the flyway boundaries have been adjusted to correspond to state lines to aid law enforcement. State game wardens and federal U. S. Game Management Agents both enforce state game laws.

Maintenance of the duck and goose populations is dependent on other factors in addition to hunting regulation. Food, of course, is of primary importance, and while grain feeding in emergency is helpful, preservation of the natural environment of the waterfowl is more important. Restoration of marsh lands, water pollution, flooding, and silting controls, help to produce areas for growth of natural plant foods.

In addition to the major plant foods, the primary animal foods include small mollusks (clams, snails, etc.), crustaceans (shrimp, barnacles, crabs, crayfish), insects and insect larvae, small fish and minnows. Other plant foods include algae, corn, sorghum, oats and other grains, sawgrass, and a large variety of aquatic plants.

RANGE MAPS

Each species has a map defining the summer or breeding range by the pattern , and a winter range indicated by ///. The bird is found throughout the year in areas where the two patterns overlap. The birds can be found outside these ranges during certain times of the year since their migration paths will join the summer and winter regions. In any case, the birds are found only in certain environments in their regions, such as marshes, woods, ponds, salt water, etc.

IMPORTANT WATERFOWL PLANT FOODS

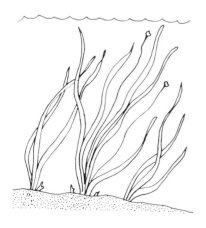

Wild Celery, *Vallisneria*
Commonly called eelgrass, this plant is widespread throughout northeastern ponds and streams. This is an extremely valuable food, and the entire plant is eaten.

9

IMPORTANT WATERFOWL PLANT FOODS

Arrowhead, *Sagittaria*
This plant, also known as duck potato, is common in swamps and along river banks. The tubers and seeds are eaten.

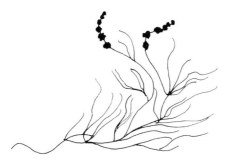

Pondweed, *Potamogeton*
All parts of this important food plant are eaten. It bears seeds and is found in fresh and brackish water.

Smartweed, *Polygonum*
This form of buckwheat is found in both marshes and higher, drier grounds. Also called knotweed; seeds are eaten.

Wild Rice, *Zizania*
The seeds of this tall grass are eaten, and it also provides excellent shelter for waterfowl in the streams and marshes where it is found.

Wild Millet, *Echinochloa*
This dense grass provides shelter as well as large seeds.

IMPORTANT WATERFOWL PLANT FOODS

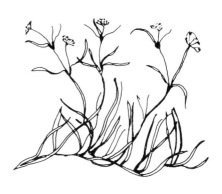

Bulrush, *Scirpus*
This plant can vary greatly in appearance and is common in ponds, streams and brackish marshes. Waterfowl eat the seeds and stems.

Widgeon Grass, *Ruppia*
This common pondweed is found in brackish coastal waters and is also known as sea grass. The entire plant is eaten.

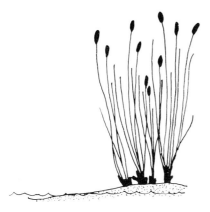

Spikerush, *Eleocharis*
The seeds and tubers of this fresh water sedge are eaten. The plant is nearly leaf-less.

Muskgrass, *Chara*
This algae is found throughout fresh and brackish waters. The entire lime-coated plant is eaten by ducks.

Cordgrass, *Spartina*
This is the primary marsh grass of the Atlantic and gulf coasts. The seeds and root stocks are eaten.

Geese

Except for brant and emperor, geese are more comfortable on land. Most of their food is obtained on land and water is used only for drinking and protection. Their bills are adapted for eating vegetable matter—grasses and grain sprouts—which grow close to the ground.

They have a longer neck, longer legs, and smaller feet than ducks. They walk and run easily without the obvious duck waddle. Also unlike ducks, male and female geese are the same color. Along with swans, geese are credited for being the most intelligent waterfowl.

All geese are strong flyers. In spite of their size, they fly almost as fast as ducks and possess great maneuverability, though not as much as ducks. However, geese have great endurance and can fly at high altitudes. They are also good swimmers and can dive adeptly when necessary.

Geese are gregarious, except during the breeding season. Male and female mate for life, taking new mates only if one partner dies or if the pair are inadvertently separated. The male guards the nest during incubation and will fight to defend the female and her clutch. After hatching, the male helps rear and protect the young, and the family remains together through the winter and migration period—almost an entire year—until the next breeding period.

Brant are much more aquatic geese and feed almost exclusively on marine vegetation, except during the nesting season. The emperor goose feeds heavily along the sea shore and eats shellfish and other marine animals.

American Brant   *Branta bernicla,* also *Branta bernicla hrota*

These geese are a salt water species which feeds on plant stems and eelgrass. They gather on sand bars along the shoreline after eating and swallow sand to aid their digestion. They are considered a good food bird.

The American brant population was seriously hurt due to a blight which destroyed the eelgrass of the east coast during the 1930's. The birds that survived did so by eating sea lettuce, a type of algae, and roots of marsh grasses and rushes. When the eelgrass recovered, the brant population built up again, but not to its original numbers.

They nest in extreme northern regions, and severe weather for any extended period of time in the breeding ground may destroy nests and most of the young birds. The nest is a hollow, lined with moss and down. The male guards the nest while the female incubates her 3-5 cream colored eggs.

The head, neck, and breast of the American brant are black. They have a white band on the sides of the neck which is broken at both the front and back of the neck. The belly is light gray, sides are whitish, and under tail coverts are white. The white neck color is absent in the immature bird. The mature bird is 22-30 inches long and 3-3½ lbs.

Black Brant   *Branta nigricans*

Black brant are a littoral species which feed on eelgrass in protected shallows along the shoreline which they inhabit. They have well developed salt glands which allow them to live completely on salt water and its vegetation. They winter on salt bays, estuaries and lakes of the western United States.

Their nests are beds of grass and down and normally will contain 4-8 buff colored eggs. The incubation period is 4 weeks and, shortly after hatching, the chicks rush to the sea.

The black brant can be distinguished from the American brant by *nigricans'* darker underside and the white collar which is unbroken at the throat. *B. nigricans* has a black head, neck, and breast; the belly is dark. The neck is marked with a white band, sides are whitish, and under tail coverts are white. An immature indivi-

13

dual will not have the white neck collar. Mature individuals range from 23-26 inches and 3-3½ lbs.

Some believe that the black brant is really a Pacific sub-species of the American brant and the scientific name *Branta bernicla orientales* is applied.

American brant

black brant

Barnacle Goose *Branta leucopsis*

This is basically an old world species, but it is mentioned because it is occasionally seen mixed with flocks of other geese along the east coast during fall.

Barnacle geese are coastal birds which feed on grass, leaves, and moss on shore, but never far from water.

Down-lined nests are built on cliff ledges. They contain 4-5 gray eggs which hatch in about 24 days. The young are sometimes carried down from the cliffs by the parents or they drop from the nest supported by air currents and land safely in water.

Barnacle geese have a white forehead and white face which is marked with a black line from the bill to each eye. The crown, neck, and breast are all black; the belly is white, and the gray back is marked with bars. They average 26 inches in length and 3-3½ lbs.

Canada Goose *Branta canadensis*

This is the most widely distributed goose species and consists of 11 races, or sub-species, ranging in size from 5-18 lbs.

Except for size, all sub-species are similar in appearance. The larger sub-species have a wing span to six feet and are commonly called "honkers" because of their characteristic call. The smaller races have a cackling call and are nicknamed "cacklers".

The Canada geese feed on waste grain, shoots of new crops, and sometimes roots of aquatic plants.

They migrate in an extended V-pattern with each goose separated enough from the others so that all birds have an unobstructed front view. When the migrating flocks set down to feed, one or two of the geese stand watch, and if danger is noticed, the flock can take off in an instant of the warning call. Although many Canada geese migrate to wildlife refuges, they are capable of flying as much 4000 miles during migration.

15

RACES OF CANADA GOOSE

LARGE SUB-SPECIES

giant Canada goose *B. c. maxima* Largest of the species, 10-18 lbs., which at one time was presumed to be extinct, but is still occasionally taken by hunters.

western Canada goose *B. c. moffitti* Larger members are 12-13 lbs.

Todd's or interior Canada goose *B. c. interior* Weighs 7-13 lbs. and is the most numerous sub-species and is found predominently in the central states.

Atlantic Canada goose *B. c. canadensis* 7-13 lbs.

Vancouver Canada goose *B. c. fulva* 7-13 lbs.

MEDIUM SUB-SPECIES

dusky Canada goose *B. c. occidentalis* 4-8 lbs.

lesser Canada goose *B. c. parvipes* 4-8 lbs.

SMALL SUB-SPECIES

Taverner's Canada goose *B. c. taverneri* 3½-5½ lbs.

Aleutian Canada goose *B. c. leucopareia* 3½-5½ lbs.

Richardson's Canada goose *B. c. hutchinsi* 3½-5½ lbs.

cackling Canada goose *B. c. minima* 2½-4 lbs.

The Canada goose breeds in the same place where it hatched. This often results in inbreeding and thus the distinctive characteristics of various nesting colonies. Two year old ganders will fight over a female; the victor wins his mate for life.

The larger races breed the farthest south. Breeding areas are forests or fields near marshes or rivers. Here the nest is made of grass and sticks and is built on an islet or on a beaver lodge. In the northwest, they breed on cliff ledges or use empty osprey nests. In the far north, the smaller sub-species breed on islets on the tundra. The nest is built in a hollow and is lined with grass and down.

The male constantly guards the female and her 5-6 cream colored eggs during the 28-30 day incubation period. Within 48 hours after hatching, the yellow-green goslings parade after father and mother to the water to feed. Both parents care for the young—others as well as their own. The young are flightless until they grow wing feathers. The adults molt after nesting and are flightless for about a month.

The Canada goose has a black head and neck, white "cheeks" and "chin", white tail coverts and belly. The feet are black, back is gray-brown to dark brown, and the breast is gray to brown. Mature individuals range from 22-43 inches and 5-18 lbs.

Snow Goose   *Chen hyperborea*

The snow goose has two sub-species—the lesser snow goose, which is one of the most abundant geese, and the less populous greater snow goose. There is speculation that the lesser snow goose is really a color phase of the blue goose.

The lesser snow goose breeds on the arctic coast of Alaska and migrates to the Mississippi valley and the west. The greater migrates from the breeding grounds in Greenland and northeast Canada to the Atlantic coast, and to coastal salt marshes where they feed on marsh grass.

The moss- and down-lined nest is a depression in the tundra, and holds 4-8 white eggs.

Both sub-species are white. They have black-tipped wings, a pink bill and feet, and the head is often rusty. The young are light gray and have a dark bill. They have a honking call. Adults are 23-38 inches long and the lesser snow goose weighs 4-6 lbs., while the greater snow goose is 6-10 lbs.

Ross' Goose   *Chen rossii*, also *Anser rossi*

This smallest and rarest of the North American geese is very similar to the snow goose and is often found with them. *C. rossii* is much smaller than the snow goose and its bill is shorter and lacks dark markings. The immature Ross' goose is lighter gray than the young snow goose.

They eat grass shoots and waste grain. They nest in the Perry River region of the arctic where the nest is built of willow twigs and lined with grass and down. The goose lays 2-6 white eggs.

These small, white geese have black-tipped

wings and a reddish bill with a warty nose. They are 21-15 inches long—about the size of mallard ducks. Their call is a weak, grunting noise.

Canada goose

snow goose

Blue Goose *Chen caerulescens,* also *Chen caerulescens caerulescens,* also *Anser caerulescens caerulescens*

The blue goose and the lesser snow goose breed in the same areas. Interbreeding has occured producing both dark and white offspring. The population of blues has become more abundant in recent years, which has led scientists to believe that the young blues have a higher survival rate since, even though they breed in the same area, they breed at a later date than the lesser snow goose.

Scientists also speculate that the lesser snow goose and the blue goose are merely color phases of the same species, which has led to the inconsistent and interchanged use of the scientific name.

The blue goose nests on the tundra. The nests, which contain 3-5 white eggs, are made of moss and grass and are lined with down. The primary food of the blue goose is marsh plants.

The blue goose has a white neck and head, the latter often stained with rust. They have a gray-brown body with blue-gray and black marked wings. The immature bird has a gray head and neck. Adults are 23-38 inches long and weigh 4½-7 lbs.

White-fronted Goose *Anser albifrons frontalis*

There are several sub-species of "speckle-belly", as the white-fronted goose is often called. One of these races is very rare and is known as the tule goose, *A. a. gambelli,* and while it resembles *frontalis,* it is darker and often as much as 10 lbs. heavier. Nesting grounds of the tule goose are unknown, but the white-fronted goose, along with two other races, breeds in the arctic.

The whitefront has a loud laugh-like call which has given him another nickname, "laughing goose". They are very agile and extremely fast flyers. During migrations, the precise V formations are led by old ganders. The nest of the whitefront is constructed of grass and normally holds 5-6 buff-colored eggs. The goslings are olive colored.

The white-fronted goose has a white muzzle, a pink bill which changes to blue at the base, and gray-brown underparts. The off-white breast and belly are marked with speckles of black. The feet are yellow. The young bird lacks the white face mark and the whitish belly, and resembles the blue goose except that the whitefront has yellow feet instead of dark feet. They are 26-34 inches long and weigh 5-8 lbs.

Emperor Goose *Philacte canagica,* also *Anser canagicus*

One of the most attractive yet least known of our geese, the emperor goose is a sea bird and lives within a few miles of the coast. It feeds on grass in spring like other geese. However, in winter the emperor goose feeds on mussels and other shellfish, which gives its flesh a strong flavor and odor.

In winter, a few may wander as far south as the bays of northern California, but most spend the cold months in the Aleutian Islands and the Alaskan peninsula.

They breed on Alaska's northwest coast. The ganders are very jealous and extremely protective. The nest is made of grass, moss, and down and is located on a tundra islet, in a salt marsh, or on driftwood. The 5-6 cream-colored eggs hatch into pearl-gray goslings who head for the water soon after hatching. The young develop their wing feathers very quickly, and the wing feathers of the adults are renewed quickly also, so that the entire family is airborne by early August.

The emperor goose has a white tail, white head with the white continuing down the neck. The throat is black and the blue-gray body is marked with black and white bars. The heads of young birds are gray. The emperor goose ranges from 26-28 inches and 6-7 lbs.

blue goose

white-fronted goose

emperor goose

Surface-feeding Ducks

Black ducks and mallards are the most common representatives of this group, also known as dabbling ducks. Surface-feeding ducks feed on weeds from fresh and brackish waters and occasionally on grain from fields. They are character-ized by having a bright speculum on the rear of each wing. When compared to diving ducks, the dabbling ducks have smaller feet and the hind toes do not have a wide flap or lobe. In North America, the males are usually more brightly colored except in summer after the breeding season when molting occurs and the male resembles the female. This interim color is probably protective camouflage, since they are unable to fly when the wings are molting.

They are excellent surface swimmers and most species can dive fairly well. They generally live in small shallow bodies of fresh water where food can be found without submerging. During certain periods of the year, they feed off the land. The bills of surface-feeding ducks are all quite similar. They are adapted for straining small organisms in mud and water. These strainers (lamellae) are best developed in the bills of shovelers, cinnamon teal, and blue-winged teal. The surface-feeding ducks feed by dabbling along edges of small, shallow bodies of fresh water, usually protected by reeds and grasses. In fall, a large amount of food is obtained from field remains of harvested grain. Their primary diet con-sists of vegetable matter and thus they have the best tasting flesh of all the ducks.

The wings are large relative to the body size, which enables the dabbling ducks to fly up and out quickly from their normally heavily overgrown terrain. With tremendous power, they can leap directly into the air from land or water. When taking off from water, they supply sufficient take-off speed by the initial powerful downstroke of the large wings striking the water.

Most species in this group are normally found in flocks, except in the south and southwest where Mexican and mottled ducks are found in pairs or small groups. The flocks fly together casually, only occasionally forming a V pattern. In spring and fall, the surface-feeding ducks follow precise migratory routes.

Almost all males of this group are distinctively marked. Females lack special coloring except for the female black and wood ducks. The female black duck resembles the male, and the female wood duck, although marked strikingly different than the male, is the only female duck that has iridescent plumage other than the speculum.

In captivity, surface-feeding ducks will normally keep the same mate as long as it is near. In nature, they may have new mates every year. Males generally leave females and band together in summer and autumn, lessening the chance for reuniting with a former mate. The females often return to the same nesting site year after year.

Wood Duck *Aix sponsa*

The wood duck was greatly endangered in the early part of the 20th century. Extensive logging and drainage destroyed woodland swamps along with the big hollow trees which are used for nesting by this species. They were heavily hunted and were considered prize trophies because of their handsome colors. In 1918 a law was passed to protect the wood duck, and by 1941 the wood duck, once again, became fairly common.

The female wood duck nests in the same spot year after year or in an areas where she was hatched. Hollows in trees as high as 50

feet above the ground are used as nests for the 10-15 white eggs. The bottom of the hollow where the nest is located can be as much as 6-8 feet below the opening. Their nesting habit has also given them the nickname "tree duck".

Two-day old young are able to climb to the opening of the hollow. The hatchlings are born with sharp needle-like claws and a hooked point at the tip of the bill.

In water, wood ducks feed on insects and duckweed. On land they eat acorns from the forest trees. They make a "whoo-eek" sound when alarmed or taking off into flight.

There are two populations of wood ducks. The larger population is found in the eastern half of the United States into southeastern Canada. The other group is found in the Pacific northwest, from southwest British Columbia south to the San Joaquin Valley of California.

All wood ducks are crested and have a white throat and belly. The male has a white-striped face, and the head and back are iridescent green, bronze, and purple. He has a white band in front of the wings and a spotted reddish-brown breast. The female has a gray-brown face, tan flanks, and a white patch around the eye. The female of this species is much more colorful than females of other species and she is the only one to have a considerable amount of iridescent plumage. Mature individuals are 17-20 inches and 1-1½ lbs.

Cinnamon Teal   *Anas cyanoptera septentrionalium*

Cinnamon teal are closely related and similar in behavior to the blue-winged teal. Females of the two species are almost identical in appearance, except the bill on the cinnamon teal is longer.

The grass nest is built in reeds and lined with down. The female incubates 6-12 off-white eggs and unlike most ducks, the male does not always desert the female when this period begins.

They feed in very shallow water or on banks. Their food is mainly bulrush, pondweed, saltgrass, sedge, and their animal food consists of insects and mollusks.

Two distinct populations of the cinnamon teal exist—the other is in southern South America more than 2000 miles away and there is no migration between the two groups.

The male's call is a chatter; the female quacks weakly. Male and female have a blue patch on each forewing, a green speculum with a white edge, and whitish wing lining. The male is cinnamon-red on the chest and head; the female is mottled brown. Adults range from 14½-17 inches and weigh around 1 lb.

wood duck

cinnamon teal

blue-winged teal

green-winged teal

Blue-winged Teal   *Anas discors*

The population of bluewings is concentrated in the prairie country of the United States and Canada. The nest is made of grass and down and hidden in tall grass along ponds, marshes and potholes. The clutch of 8-10 cream-colored eggs hatches in 22 days. A few hours after hatching, the mother leads the young to water. The young can fly at 6 weeks of age.

They prefer to feed in very shallow water where they eat tender parts of aquatic plants, seeds, water insects, and mollusks. Animal food makes up about 30% of their diet.

The male's call is a peep; the female's, a soft quack. Both have a blue patch on the forewing and a green speculum with one white edge. The male has a slate gray head, white face crescent, brownish back, spotted light-brown undersides and a white patch on each flank. The female is mottled brown with a whitish underside. Adults weigh around a pound and are 14-16½ inches long.

Green-winged Teal   *Anas carolinensis*

This very handsome bird is the smallest of all our waterfowl. They feed primarily on plant matter and are sought out by hunters because of their excellent tasting flesh. They eat seeds of bulrush, pondweed, sedge, and panic grass; animal food includes insects and mollusks.

The nest is placed in a hollow in high grass, usually near water. The female incubates 10-12 whitish eggs, and the male deserts her as soon as the eggs are laid.

The common teal, *Anas crecca*, a Eurasian relative, is very similar in appearance to the greenwing. The common teal lacks the white crescent on the wing, and it occasionally visits the northwest and east coasts and, more often, the Aleutians.

The voice of the male greenwing is a short whistle; the female quacks. They have a green and black speculum with a buff border, and whitish belly. The male has a chestnut head with a slight crest and a green patch. His back is gray-brown and the front of the wing is marked with a white bar. The female has a brownish back and sides. Mature individuals weigh up to 1 lb. and are 12½-15½ inches long.

Mallard *Anas platyrhynchos*

The mallard is the most abundant water-fowl in North America, and is found throughout the northern hemisphere, but less commonly in the eastern United States. It is also the ancestor of domesticated types which are raised commercially.

Mallards feed on water and marsh plants, and occasionally on grain, seeds, hickory nuts, and acorns. They are large, excellent table fare.

The nest, made of grass and down, is hidden among reeds on dry ground near water. In 26 days, the 8-12 buff eggs hatch into yellow and sepia ducklings. The young are led to water as soon as they are able to walk.

During winter, mallards are heavily concentrated along the gulf coast and south Mississippi valley. Many are found in White River National Wildlife Refuge in Arkansas.

The drakes make a soft *"kwek"* noise, but the females quack loudly. Both have violet speculums bordered with black and white, and have white wing linings. The male has a green head, white collar and white outer tail feathers. The back is brown, rump is black, breast is chestnut, and the belly is gray. The female is mottled brown and has paler underparts. Mature individuals average 2-4 lbs. and 20-28 inches.

Gadwall *Anas strepera*

This uncommon duck is found most often among flocks of pintails and widgeon. Females resemble female mallards. The male gadwall has no characteristic colors—also called "gray duck"—but both sexes can be identified by the white speculum since they are the only species of dabbling duck to have this color wing patch.

They dive more than other surface-feeding ducks, but their food consists almost entirely of vegetable matter—aquatic plants, acorns, and grain. They are also good walkers and will feed in woodlands. Gadwalls are good eating ducks.   *Continued on page 31*

mallard

gadwall

They summer in the prairie regions of the northwest United States and southwest Canada and some are found nesting on the Atlantic coast. The nest is built in high grass on islands, or sometimes away from the water. Females lay 10-12 white eggs. Newly hatched young head for the water to feed on water insects.

The call of both male and female is a loud quack, higher in pitch than the female mallard. They have chestnut-colored forewings, white speculum, whitish belly and wing lining, and yellow feet. The male has a brown head, gray back and sides, and black rump. The female is a mottled-brown color. Adults are 18½-23½ inches and 2-3 lbs.

Black Duck *Anas rubripes*

The black duck is more common in the east, but the population is increasing in the western part of the United States. They winter in coastal marshes and wooded swamps; many live in the Mississippi and Great Lake drainages. They feed on mollusks in open water during the day, and in salt marshes during twilight hours.

Many migrate north in spring, but others move inland and nest near streams of fresh water ponds. Nest containing 6-12 greenish-tan eggs are hidden in grass or underbrush. The young feed on insects and the female cares for them for 8 weeks before they are abandoned.

The black duck's voice is the same as the mallard's. They have a yellowish or olive bill, gray crown, light-brown head and neck which are marked with streaks. The body is dark mottled brown, the speculum is violet and bordered in black, wing lining is white, feet are reddish-brown. Male and female are similar in appearance but can be distinguished by the markings on the breast feathers. The feathers of the male are marked with a rounded "U" pattern, whereas the female's feathers are marked with a "V". Mature individuals are 21-25 inches and 2½-3½ lbs.

Mottled Duck *Anas fulvigula*

The mottled duck is more carnivorous than other surface-feeding ducks and eats mollusks, insects, and fish in addition to its vegetable diet of aquatic plants and seeds.

The Florida or summer mallard, as it is also called, nests in salt or brakish water. The nest is lined with down and holds 8-11 greenish eggs.

The call of the mottled duck is similar to the mallard's. Female and male are similar in appearance and both resemble the female mallard, except the bill does not have the black patches of the mallard. Mottled ducks have a yellow or orange bill, brownish crown with buff face and throat. The body is mottled brown, the speculum is purple with a black border, and the wing lining is white. Adults are around 20 inches long and weigh about 2½ lbs.

black duck

mottled duck

33

Pintail *Anas acuta*

After mallards and black ducks, pintails are one of the most populous waterfowl. They have longer necks than most surface-feeding ducks which allow them to feed deeper in the water without upending. The long tail of the male is characteristic of the species and can be seen even when the pintail is sitting on water, where they feed mainly on water plants and seeds, some mollusks, and insects.

Pintails have the widest breeding range of all North American ducks and have their most common range in the west. Their nest is lined with straw and down and holds 6-10 greenish or tan eggs. After hatching, the young follow the mother to the closest body of water—sometimes as much as a mile away in prairie breeding areas. The young pintails have wing feathers and are able to fly by July.

During the fall migration, more than 1 million pintails fly to the Sacramento National Wildlife Refuge in California. Others head for interior fresh water marshes and brackish coastal marshes.

The rare Bahama duck, *Anas bahamensis,* which is sometimes found in the southeast and West Indies, resembles the female pintail. But the Bahama duck is smaller, only 13 inches, and has white markings on the tail and cheeks, and has a mottled-red bill.

The pintail's call is a short whistle. Both sexes have a greenish-bronze speculum with a white border on one edge. The male has a brown head, white throat, white stripes on the neck and breast, a gray back, and long, thin tail. The female is mottled brown and has a short pointed tail. Adults are 20-30 inches long and weigh 1¾-3½ lbs.

Mexican Duck *Anas diazi*

This is a rare duck whose range is restricted to a small area and its identity is often confused with the female mallard. However, the female Mexican duck is slightly darker and has a brighter bill—without dark markings —than the female mallard.

The Mexican duck breeds in swamp thickets of the upper Rio Grande Valley and in the marshes of southwest New Mexico. The nest is built in thick sedge or rushes and contains 5-9 greenish eggs.

Both sexes have a mottled brown body, purple speculum with black and white borders. The male has a yellow-green bill and the female has an orange bill. Mature Mexican ducks average 20-22 inches and weigh around 2 lbs.

American Widgeon   *Mareca americana,* also *Anas americana*

These ducks relish roots of water celery and other deep aquatic plants, but since they do not dive they often steal these foods from diving ducks. American widgeon normally feed in shallow water, but sometimes graze in grain or alfalfa fields.

"Baldpates"—named for the white crown of the drakes—nest in a hollow on weed covered islets or on a grassland away from water. The nest of leaves and down holds 9-11 creamy-white eggs which hatch in 24-25 days.

The male's call is a soft whistle, usually sounded 3 times in quick succession; the female makes an unmelodious croak. Both sexes have a gray neck, small blue bill, white patch on forewing, green and black speculum, and a whitish belly. Drakes have a white crown and flank patch, iridescent green head patch, and a pinky-brown body. The female has a gray head and brown body. Adults are 16½-20 inches and 1½-2½ lbs.

European Widgeon   *Mareca penelope*

Small numbers of this Old World species are regular visitors to the northern coasts of North America in fall. They are usually found in flocks with the American widgeon.

They are known to breed in Europe and Asia on farmlands, but if they breed in North America, their nesting grounds are not known. The nest is made of grass and down and contains 7-8 off-white eggs.

The call of the European widgeon is a high, descending whistle. Both sexes are similar to the American widgeon—they have a white patch on the forewing and a green speculum. However, the male European has a buff crown, chestnut head and neck, and gray back; the female has a browner head than the American and has a grayish wing lining. Adults average 16½-20 inches and 1½-2 lbs.

pintail

American widgeon

European widgeon

Shoveler *Spatula clypeata,* also *Anas clypeata*

Except for the large, spoon-shaped bill, the shoveler resembles the blue-winged teal. The bill of the shoveler is equipped with lamellae, comb-like teeth, which strain larvae and small crustaceans from the mud the "spoonbill" feeds in.

Nests are built in a pond or slough, and the 6-12 eggs are buff or gray colored. The newly hatched young have normal size and shape bills, but they change to the distinctive shoveler shape in just two weeks.

Shovelers make a low clucking sound or a quack similar to a mallard. Male and female have a huge bill, blue wing patch, green speculum with a white border, orange legs, and white wing lining. The male has a blackish-green head and rump, white chest, upper back and flank patch. His belly and sides are chestnut colored. The female is mottled brown. Mature individuals are 17-20 inches and weigh 1½-2 lbs.

Tree Ducks

In spite of their name, not all tree ducks are arboreal. Both sexes of tree ducks look alike. Their long legs and long necks give them a goose-like appearance.

Tree ducks feed at night preferably on corn, but they will eat seeds and acorns. They would rather wade than swim, and they do not dive. The call of tree ducks is a shrill whistle.

Fulvous Tree Duck   *Dendrocygna bicolor*

This "whistling duck" does not nest in trees and rarely perches in them. The fulvous tree duck is found in marshland rice fields and ponds but is seldom seen due to its nocturnal feeding habits.

The species has the characteristic long neck and goose-like appearance; the legs project beyond the tail during flight making the fulvous tree duck easy to identify. They nest in high marsh grasses of coastal Texas and Louisiana, and unlike most waterfowl, the nest is *not* lined with down. A single clutch will consist of 12-14 eggs, but nests containing more than 30 eggs can be found, since more than one female may use the same "dump nest". Even though there may be more than one duck per nest, the eggs may still go unattended.

Male and female are alike and have a tawny-brown colored head and underparts, black on the rump, a cream-colored side stripe, and white patch on the rump. Mature individuals are 18-21 inches and under 2 lbs.

Black-bellied Tree Duck   *Dendrocygna autumnalis*

Populous in Mexico, the *pato maizal* (cornfield duck) as it is called there, has only limited areas of its natural breeding habitat still undestroyed in southern Texas. The species can only be found along the banks of the Rio Grande in the Santa Ana National Wildlife Refuge and sometimes in Arizona and California.

This tree duck perches in trees and builds its nest in a tree cavity in brush country. A clutch will contain 12-16 white eggs.

This species has unusually large wings and a loud clear whistle. The black-bellied tree duck has a coral bill, gray face, red-brown crown, neck and breast. The wings are black with a white patch, the belly is black, and the long legs are pink. Adults are 20-22 inches and weigh around 2 lbs.

shoveler

fulvous tree duck

Diving Ducks

Diving ducks are divided into four groups known as sub-families or tribes: pochard group (tribe *Aythini*) includes the canvasback, redhead, ring-necked duck, the scaups; tribe *Mergini* includes the goldeneyes, bufflehead, oldsquaw, scoters, harequin, and mergansers; tribe *Somaterini* includes the eiders; and the stiff-tailed duck group (tribe *Oxyorini*), the ruddy duck.

Diving ducks can be distinguished from surface-feeding ducks by their legs and feet. The legs on diving ducks are located farther back and farther apart than the dabblers', the feet are larger and have large lobes on the hind toes. This leg location and foot size restricts the movement of the diving ducks on land— thus these species are seldom seen out of water.

Much of their lives are spent at sea where they dive for food. The normal diving depth is 15 feet, but some species can dive to 180 feet. They usually remain submerged for about 90 seconds, but they can survive underwater for 15-16 minutes if circumstances require. Some diving ducks, such as mergansers and buffleheads, are able to swim underwater at such great speed that they can catch swimming fish.

Diving ducks have more variety in the shape and size of their bills that the dabbling ducks. Generally, their bills are shorter and wider, but the goldeneye has a bill similar to the surface-feeding ducks, whereas the scoters and eiders have heavy bills capable of crushing small shellfish.

Their wing beat is more rapid than that of the dabblers, but they do not possess as great maneuverability in flight.

The males desert the females when incubation begins, grouping together on open water to moult, but, unlike dabblers, they do not hide during their flightless period. Like the dabbling ducks, diving females abandon the young before they are able to fly, in order to hide during their own flightless molting period.

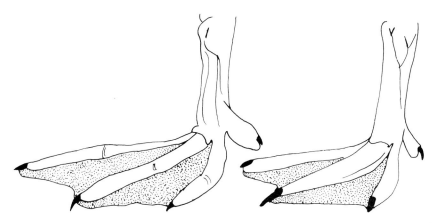

The foot of the diving duck (left) is larger and has a large lobe on the hind toe compared to the foot of a dabbling duck (right).

Males and females are marked and colored differently. Females are brownish overall; males, except the canvasback, have some iridescent plumage, but none of the diving ducks have iridescent speculums.

The pochards are more closely related to the dabbling ducks than are the other divers. They are generally found on fresh water, but will protect themselves in winter in coastal bays and river mouths, and the redhead and greater scaup will frequent coastal waters during winter. These species dive from the surface and swim under water, and eat more animal food than the surface-feeding ducks. Pochards are large, heavy birds that run along the surface of the water to gain speed for take-off. Generally, their calls are short, low-pitched croaks.

The mergansers have a highly specialized bill which is slender, cylindrical, and serrated—well suited for seizing and holding live fish. They do not threaten fish populations, even though they are sometimes charged. These large but streamlined fresh water birds dive and swim quickly, and have smaller wings (than the dabbling ducks), which do not interfere with diving. However, the wings still provide efficient flight assuming some take-off speed is generated by pattering off the water surface for some distance. Nine species of these "fish ducks" occur in the northern hemisphere, but only three in North America.

Like the mergansers, goldeneyes are expert divers and are actually capable of catching live fish. Although most breed on or near fresh water, goldeneyes, along with eiders, scoters, buffleheads, oldsquaw, and harlequins, are the ducks most generally associated with salt water.

The eiders are the hardiest of the diving ducks. Their range is in the extreme north, restricted only by the availability of open water. They are strictly sea birds, except during the breeding season.

The ruddy duck is an excellent diver, but is almost helpless on land. It is characterized by the long, stiff tail which is often held vertically or pointed toward the head. Several females may lay eggs in a common nest, and one or two may end up mothering 30-40 ducklings. On occasion, males help with the young instead of disappearing as do males of other species.

Redhead *Aythya americana*

Redheads are often found in the company of canvasbacks and scaups. They migrate mainly along the Pacific and central flyways in V-shaped flocks, but fly in irregular bunches or lines on shorter flights. In winter, the largest concentration is found along the southern Texas coast.

They have a higher vegetable content diet than other diving ducks—about 90% vegetable matter. Redheads eat leaves and stems of aquatic plants, dive for other vegetation, and also feed in shallows on water insects and small shellfish.

A great number breed in potholes and sloughs of undrained northern prairie lands. Nests are made of matted grasses and are built in rushes near deep water. The 10-15 creamy eggs hatch in 22-24 days. Females may use other "dump nests" for their eggs.

Their call is a strange loud quack, similar to the meowing of a cat. Redheads have a blue bill with black tip and whitish wing patch. The male has a brownish-red head and neck, a black rump, chest and tail; the back is gray and undersides are white. The female is brown and has a light face patch near the bill. Adults average 18-22 inches and 2-3½ lbs.

Canvasback *Aythya valisineria*

Cans, as they are called, resemble the redhead but are larger, have a long neck, and their backs are very white. Once quite common, these birds are no longer plentiful due to heavy hunting and drought. They make one of the best table birds if they have been eating the right diet. However, they taste awful if they have been feeding on rotting salmon and shellfish in the Pacific northwest. Their normal diet is 80% vegetarian, primarily wild celery *Vallisneria* (thus the cans' species name) in winter, with snails and crustaceans making up the balance. They can dive as deep as 30 feet for plants.

Canvasbacks are one of the fastest flying ducks, with speeds of 70 mph. They fly in V-formation during migration, but flock in tight bunches on shorter flights.

They nest in sloughs and ponds among rushes and cattails in the prairie regions of central Canada. The nest is a platform of intertwined plants and holds 7-9 greenish-gray eggs. If their nesting area is dry due to drought, the cans do not breed. The males have a less complete and much shorter eclipse molt than other species, and have their complete breeding plumage by the beginning of November.

Canvasbacks are characterized by their long sloping head and long dark bill. The male has a brownish-red head and neck, black breast, and white body. The female is brown on the head, neck and breast, and has a grayish body. Mature individuals are 19½-24 inches and 2½-3½ lbs.

redhead

canvasback

44

lesser scaup

greater scaup

Lesser Scaup   *Aythya affinis*

The greater and lesser scaups are very similar in size and appearance. The lesser is only slightly smaller and if viewed in sunlight, generally has a purple tone to the head while the greater has a green cast. The head color is not reliable since both scaups appear black in poor lighting.

The "little bluebills" are the most abundant diving duck along the Mississippi flyway. Their breeding area is concentrated in Canadian prairie sloughs, where the grass and down-lined nest is built on the ground, usually close to water. The clutch normally consists of 9-12 olive-tan eggs. The lesser scaup winters on inland waters.

They are expert divers and feed on pondweed, snails and water insects with animal matter making up about 40% of their diet.

Their call sounds like a loud "scaup". The lesser scaup has a blue bill, white breast, a white stripe on the wing which is shorter than the one on the greater scaup, since only the secondary wing feathers are marked with white. The male has a black head and neck with a purple gloss. His back is whitish, sides are gray, tail and chest are black. The female is brown and has a white face and belly. Adults are 15-18 inches and $1\frac{3}{4}$-$2\frac{1}{2}$ lbs.

Greater Scaup   *Aythya marila*

The "big bluebills" are common, but are outnumbered by the lesser scaup. They are usually heavier and have broader bills than the lesser, but these differences can be very small.

They are good divers and can remain under water for a long time. They eat shellfish and wild celery and grasses near shore—about 55% of their diet is animal matter.

The greater scaup breeds in the arctic regions of Alaska and northern Canada where the nest is built in hollows near ponds on the tundra. The nest holds 7-10 olive-tan eggs. They spend the winter along the Pacific coast from southern Alaska to California, and along the coast of the middle Atlantic and Gulf states, and eastern Great Lakes.

Like the lesser scaup, the voice is a loud "scaup". They have a blue bill and long white stripe on the wing (which includes white markings on the 6-7 inner wing primary feathers in addition to the white-marked secondaries). The male has a black head and neck with a greenish cast, white back and sides, and a black chest and tail. The female is brown with a white face and belly. Mature individuals are 16-20 inches and 2-3 lbs.

Ring-necked Duck   *Aythya collaris*

The ring around the neck is rather inconspicuous while the light rings around the dark bill are easily seen, giving the basis for the name "ring bill", which is also applied to this species.

Ringnecks are commonly found in woodland ponds where they feed in shallow water, but they can dive to 40 feet if necessary. They are primarily vegetarians, 80% of their diet is plant matter, thus they are usually good eating ducks. Animal foods include insects and snails.

They breed in reeds along bogs and ponds north of the prairies in western Canada. The grassy nest is built over water or at the edge of a pond, and normally contains 8-12 olive-tan eggs. Ringnecks are more confined to fresh water in winter than are other bay ducks and spend this season throughout the coastal areas of the United States, and throughout Mexico and the West Indies.

Ringnecks can rise from the water more easily than other pochards and are good flyers.

Both sexes have a peaked crown, a bill with two whitish rings, and a light-gray speculum. The male has a black head, chest and back, chestnut neck ring, and white wedge on the sides. The wings, belly and tail are dark. The female has white eye rings; back is brown, undersides are white. Adults are 14½-18 inches, 1½-2½ lbs.

Bufflehead   *Bucephala albeola*

Buffleheads are the smallest of the diving ducks. Their small size along with the white patch on their relatively large head identify both male and female. Their oversize head was the source of their name "buffalo head" which has been shortened to their present name.

Their diet consists of fish, shrimp, mussels, which make up 80% of their food—they are poor table fare. They spend summers on lakes and rivers in woodland areas, spending little time on land, even though they can walk fairly well. They can take off into flight directly
Continued on page 50

47

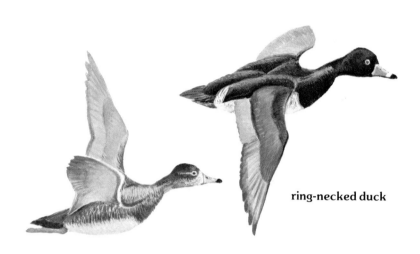

ring-necked duck

bufflehead

common goldeneye

Barrow's goldeneye

from the water surface or even from beneath without running as do other diving ducks.

Buffleheads breed primarily in the woods of northwestern Canada and build their nests in trees in old large woodpecker holes, or abandoned flicker nests in aspen trees, or sometimes in holes along banks if trees are not available. The nest is a bed of wood dust, down, and often flicker feathers, at the base of the hole and contains 10-12 ivory eggs. The young eat insect larvae and nymphs.

Buffleheads have white wing patches and a large head relative to their small size. The male has a black iridescent head with a large white crown, a black back, and white undersides. The female is gray and has a pale breast and white cheeks. Their size ranges 13-15½ inches and up to 1-1/3 lbs.

Common Goldeneye   *Bucephala clangula*, also *Bucephala americana*

The American goldeneye, as this species is also known, is commonly found in lakes and rivers in wooded areas. They feed in deeper waters than the pochards and are expert divers and even search under submerged rocks for food. Their diet consists of 75% animal food including crustaceans, insects, and mollusks; they are not good table fare.

They migrate in relatively small flocks and fly at high altitudes. However, if ponds stay ice free in winter, this species does not migrate.

The majority nest north of the Canadian border in a tree cavity or rotting stump near water. Ducks lay 8-12 greenish eggs and cover them with a heavy layer of down.

The whirring sound of their wings during flight is the source of another common name, "whistler".

The common goldeneye has white wing patches. The male has a green-black head, high crown, white face patch and undersides, and a black back. The female has a brown head, white collar, and gray body. Mature individuals are 16-20 inches and 2-3 lbs.

50

Barrow's Goldeneye *Bucephala islandica*

There are two distinct, but identical, populations of this noisy species of goldeneye. The eastern bird, which is not as abundant as the other population, breeds in the Labrador peninsula and western Greenland and winters along the Atlantic coast from St. Lawrence to Long Island. The larger population breeds and nests in the western mountains and as far south as central Colorado, and during the winter can be found on the Pacific coast as far south as San Francisco Bay.

Nests are built in cavities of decaying trees near a pond or lake. If trees are not available, the nest can be found in a rocky crevice, hole in a stream bank, or other shelter. The clutch consists of 6-15 pale green eggs.

Barrow's goldeneye feeds in fresh water on pondweed, water insects, crayfish, and other crustaceans. Approximately 75% of their diet is animal matter, so these ducks are not good eating.

Male and female have white wing patches. The male has a purple-black head with a white face crescent—which distinguishes it from the common goldeneye, white underparts, and a black body. The female has a brown head and white collar, and gray body. In spring and early summer, the female can be distinguished from the common goldeneye by her completely yellow bill—not black with a yellow tip as is the common's. Mature individuals are 16½-20 inches and weigh 1½-2½ lbs.

Oldsquaw *Clangula hyemalis*

These noisy and very hardy winter ducks were given their name by fur traders and Indians because of their constant chatter.

Their diet is 90% animal food, which includes mollusks and crustaceans. Oldsquaws are extremely good divers and can go to depths of 180-200 feet to find shellfish.

Oldsquaws are the most abundant arctic duck and breed north of the tree line around the globe. The nest, which will contain 5-7 olive-buff eggs, is built in a rock depression at the base of clumps of dwarf willows, or some nest on low maritime islands with eiders and terns.

The male oldsquaw is brownish-black with white eye patches, white flanks and belly, and has a long, sharply-pointed tail. In winter, the drake has a white head, neck and shoulders, a dark face patch, back and breast. The female has a dark crown, face patch and back; the whitish head and underparts are paler in winter. Adults are 15-22 inches and 1-2¼ lbs.

oldsquaw

harlequin

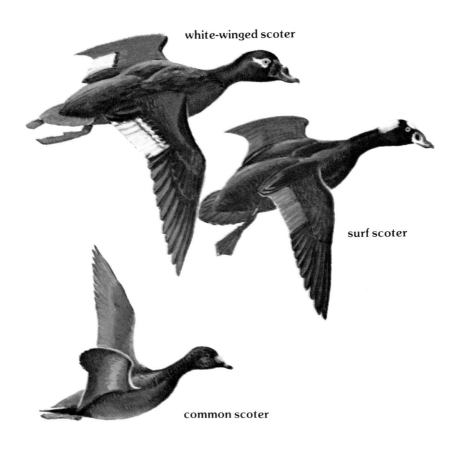

white-winged scoter

surf scoter

common scoter

Harlequin   *Histrionicus histrionicus*

There are two populations of harlequin, both of which spend most of their lives on the ocean, but breed inland. Both the Atlantic and Pacific (larger) populations are rough weather and rough terrain birds. They are not good game since their diet is almost entirely animal—insects, crustaceans, and mollusks.

These uncommon ducks can walk well on land, unlike most diving ducks. They also can bound into flight from below the water surface.

In summer, they breed near swift rivers

and along arctic shores. The nest is built on the ground in a rock cavity or in low, hollow stumps. The duck lays 6-7 buff-colored eggs. The young join the parents at the ocean as soon as they are able to fly. They winter in heavy surf off rocky coasts.

The male harlequin is gray-blue with a black crown, reddish-brown sides, and is marked with white patches throughout. The female is gray-brown and has three white patches on the sides of the head. These small ducks are 14½-21 inches and weigh 1-2 lbs.

Common Scoter *Oidemia nigra*

In spite of the name, the "black coot" is the rarest of the scoters. They feed over reefs, diving for mussels, barnacles, and limpets, which comprise 90% of their diet. Occasionally they feed on and damage commercial oyster and scallop beds.

Their nest is built in a hollow in tall grasses in the high sands of Bering Sea beaches. The nest is lined with plant material and holds 6-10 buff eggs.

The drakes have a bell-like whistle, while the females utter a harsh croak. The male is completely black (including feet) except for the yellow protuberance at the base of the black bill and the silver wing linings. The female is a dark, dusky brown on the crown and body, and has gray cheeks and throat marked with brown flecks. Mature birds are 17-20½ inches and weigh 1¾-2¾ lbs.

Surf Scoter *Melanitta perspicillata*

This is the most widely distributed scoter and is also known as the "skunkhead coot" because of the white patches on the head.

They dive and feed on shellfish and the surf scoter earned its name from its habit of feeding on the breaking surf.

The nest is a grass and down-lined depression in bushes near a lake or pond, and holds 5-9 buff eggs.

The surf scoter is smaller than the white-winged scoter, has a thick neck, and reddish feet. The male has white patches on the forehead and nape, and red and black patches on a heavy white bill. The brown female has two prominent white spots on each side of the face. Adults are 17-21 inches and 2-2½ lbs.

White-winged Scoter *Melanitta deglandi*

This largest scoter is also called "sea coot". They eat insects, pondweed, and dive to search for mussels, oysters, and scallops—animal matter makes up 94% of their diet.

They nest near prairie ponds and forest lakes, or on the tundra. The nest is lined with leaves and twigs and hidden under bushes, and contains 9-14 pinky-tan eggs.

The white-winged scoter is a large bird, has a thick neck, swollen bill, white wing patch on each wing, and reddish feet. The male is dark and has a white eye patch and orange bill with a black protuberance at the base. The female is dusky brown and has two light patches on the side of the face. Adult whitewings are 19-23½ inches and 2¾-4 lbs.

Common Eider *Somateria mollissima*

The common eider is a very important commercial duck since the gray eiderdown from the breast is used as insulation for cold weather gear and fine bedding.

The population was severly reduced by over-hunting, but has been replenished since the birds came under the protection of the Migratory Bird Treaty and since 1938, when Hudson's Bay Company built eider farms to collect the valuable down from nests.

The common eider normally breeds in dense colonies on ground on flat islets in coastal waters. They use artificial nest sites—shallow pits in the ground, crevices in stone walls—but the nesting site is always close to salt water. The down-lined nest is made of plant material and hidden by a clump of grass, and holds 4-6 olive eggs. Newly hatched ducklings go immediately to sea. An immature or unmated "babysitter" duck will watch over several broods of hatchlings.

The common eider is the largest of the diving ducks, and the only one that flies by alternately flapping the wings and sailing through the air. They dive over reefs and shoals to feed on crabs, sea urchins, and mollusks. The common eider can swallow whole shellfish up to 2 inches long, which are ground up by powerful stomach muscles. Because of their diet, common eiders have extremely fishy tasting flesh and are not good eating.

There are six races of common eider; three of the sub-species are found in North America: the American common eider, *S. m. dresseri;* the Pacific com-

common eider

king eider

Steller's eider

mon eider, *S. m. V-nigra;* and the northern common eider, *S. m. borealis.* The only distinctions among the three sub-species are small differences in bill shape and color, and head markings.

The common eider is a very large duck. The male has a white head and back, black crown and belly. The female is a rich brown with many bars or stripes. Mature individuals are 23-27 inches long and 4½-6 lbs.

King Eider   *Somateria spectabilis*

The king either spends most of its life on open sea and seldom enters sheltered waters, even in winter. They dive over reefs for crabs, shrimp, and sea urchins, which make up 95% of their diet.

They nest on a mossy tundra away from the shoreline, but near pond edges and banks of streams. The down-lined nest holds 4-7 olive-tan eggs.

This species is rare in the United States, but common in far northern North America. The name is believed to be derived from an Eskimo word *kingalik*, which means "he has a nose". Eskimos delight in eating this fatty knob off the duck's bill.

The male king eider has an orange bill and shield above the bill, a white crown, neck and breast, large white wing patch, greenish cheeks, and black back and belly. The female is brown and heavily marked with black bars. King eiders are 18½-25 inches and 3¼-4½ lbs.

Steller's Eider   *Polysticta stelleri*

This is the smallest species of eider and is quite abundant within its range. Like the other eiders, they dive for mollusks and other small marine animals.

They nest on the tundra, usually near water. The 6-10 green eggs are covered with dark brown down. The male remains near the nest but does not incubate the eggs or help with the young.

Male and female have a purple speculum. The male has a white head with a green lump on top, a black throat and back, and reddish underparts. The female is mottled brown and has white wing linings. Steller's eiders are 17-18½ inches and weigh around 2 lbs.

Spectacled Eider *Lampronetta fischeri*

The spectacled eider is rare in North America. It breeds on the tundra of river deltas of Alaska and builds its nest in a clump of grass or on a knoll near a pond, but never more than two miles inland. The nest is lined with plant material and breast down and holds 5-9 olive-tan eggs.

They feed on insects, pondweed, cranberries, and dive for mollusks. They eat more vegetable matter than other eiders, but animal matter still makes up 75% of their diet.

The male has a green head, and white eye patch, neck and back, and black underparts. The female is brown and marked with bars and has a pale brown eye patch. Adults are 20-22½ inches and 3½-3¾ lbs.

Ruddy Duck *Oxyura jamaicensis*

The ruddy duck is common in summer on lakes and ponds and during winter on estuaries, lakes, and rivers. It has at least 60 different nicknames including "booby coot" and "stifftail".

They eat pondweed seeds and stems and dive for wild celery and mollusks—vegetable matter comprises 75% of their diet.

Ruddy ducks are almost helpless on land. In water they have difficulty getting airborne, but they have the ability to submerge without diving and often use this technique as a means of escape.

Some ducks lay the first of their eggs in nests of other species. They may construct loose nests, but will abandon the eggs laid in them. The permanent nest is a woven platform of vegetation several inches above shallow water, attached to vertical stems as support. The clutch is 6-10 very large white eggs which hatch in 21 days.

Ruddy ducks are small, have white cheeks, and a stiff tail. The male is capable of holding his tail erect and has two complete plumages. The male is rust-red with a black crown, and blue bill—but he is gray in winter. The female is gray with a dark stripe on each cheek. A closely related tropical species, the masked duck, *Oxyura dominica,* sometimes enters the United States across the Rio Grande, and can be distinguished from the ruddy duck by the white wing patches of the masked duck. The ruddy duck is 14½-16 inches and 1-1¾ lbs.

spectacled eider

ruddy duck

60

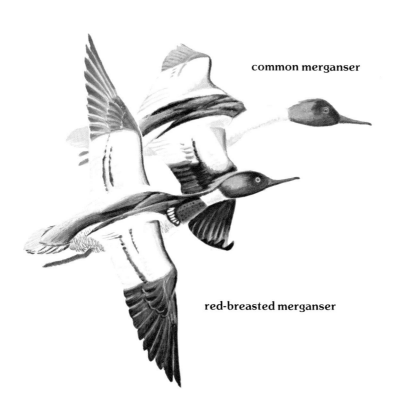

common merganser

red-breasted merganser

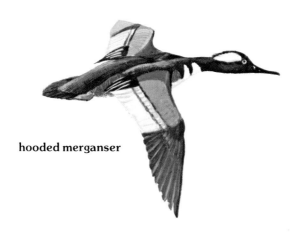

hooded merganser

Hooded Merganser *Lophodytes cucullatus,* also
Mergus cucullatus

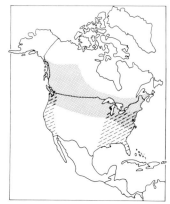

The hooded merganser is uncommon and the smallest of the mergansers. It is also the only species of this group which is found only in North America.

They breed mainly in low wet woods of the northern and eastern states, and west and southern Canada. Often they compete with wood ducks for tree cavities and sometimes they end up sharing the same nesting chamber, with each hen incubating her clutch in shifts. The 6-18 glossy-white round eggs hatch in 30 days. The young float to the ground from trees at heights as much as 75 feet. If trees are not available, the hen will nest in the shelter of a overhanging bank or stump near the shoreline. The ducklings will pack together in a compact group on the water to deceive predators.

The hooded merganser is a fast, agile flyer and can easily become airborne off the water's surface. They feed off woodland waterways and occasionally prairie sloughs, where they dive for insects and small fish, tadpoles, crustaceans. Animal matter makes up 98% of their diet.

The call of the hooded merganser is a low-pitched short quack. Both sexes have a white speculum. The male has a black-bordered white crest on top of the head, a black face and neck, white breast with two black bars in front of each wing, and brown sides. The female is brownish-gray with a white breast and has bushy buff-colored crest. Hooded mergansers are 16-19 inches and 1¼-2 lbs.

Common Merganser *Mergus merganser*

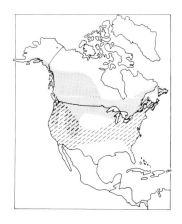

The common merganser is a common species, but it is primarily a fresh water bird and is seldom found in salt water.

Their breeding grounds are in northern evergreen forest, where the nest is built in a tree cavity, sometimes as high as 100 feet from the ground. The nesting area is always located close to a brook or a lake, and the duck lays 9-12 buff-colored eggs.

Common mergansers make a low-pitched short quack. Both sexes have a pinkish breast, and white wing patch. The male has a greenish-black head, black back, but seldom shows a crest—unlike the female and other mergansers. The female is gray with a red-brown crest on the head and has a white throat. Mature individuals are 22-27 inches and weigh 2¾-4 lbs.

Red-breasted Merganser   *Mergus serrator*

"Sawbill" spends much of its life in salt water. Redbreasts gather in flocks composed of hundreds of birds, around river mouths, in channels of salt water marshes, or off sandy shores beyond the reach of waves.

They breed in northern forests and on the edges of tundras. The nest is on the ground, protected under a log or dwarf evergreen near salt water. The 8-10 olive-tan eggs hatch in 26-28 days.

Red-breasted mergansers have a very low, toneless call. The birds are crested and have white speculums. The male has a green and black head, black back, rusty-red breast, and white collar. The female is gray and has a reddish head—similar in appearance to the common merganser but lacking contrast between the head and the throat. Redbreasts are 19½-26 inches and 2-3 lbs.

Index

Bold numbers refer to photos.